No Worries: How to Survive Australians

Robert Treborlang is admirably qualified to write on the problems of surviving Australians. He understands the principles of passivity, is highly apologetic and never asks any questions. Satirist and social critic, Treborlang has realized that Australians aren't so much a people, more a state of mind. This handbook will help you learn to cope with the "Australians" in our midst.

No Worries

HOW TO SURVIVE AUSTRALIANS

ROBERT TREBORLANG

Illustrations by Mark Knight

ANGUS
& ROBERTSON
PUBLISHERS

To the highly unusual and witty Moi Moi

ANGUS & ROBERTSON PUBLISHERS

16 Golden Square, London W1R 4BN,
United Kingdom and
PO Box 5576, Wellesley Street,
Auckland, New Zealand

First published in the United Kingdom by
Angus & Robertson (UK) in 1988
First published in New Zealand by
Angus & Robertson in 1988

Copyright © Robert Treborlang 1988

British Library Cataloguing in Publication Data
Treborlang, Robert
  No worries: how to survive Australians
  1. Australia social life – Humour
  I. Title
  994.06'3'0207

ISBN 0 207 15858 4

Printed in Great Britain by
Hazell Watson and Viney Ltd.

Contents

Induction

One brilliantly sunny day I realised I was in Australia. I found myself wandering in the streets. After two hours of walking past innumerable houses with parched gardens, I began to feel uneasy. There was no one in sight.

After some more walking, I heard the drone of human voices and the clink of glasses coming from a corner building. I stepped inside a half-opened door. I saw a row of men standing with their backs to the street and facing a wall, as if waiting to be shot. Later on I was to learn that the place was called a "pub" and that, far from being in any danger, the establishment was a spot where these men felt safe from the women persons in their lives.

Turning to the nearest group of men, I assailed them with questions about this brand new country. I did not know whether it was my clumsy manner or my odd appearance, but after a short period of questioning, the men became angry and told me to mind my own business. Not quite understanding, I asked them to elucidate. Their answer was to turn their backs.

I knew then that I would have to learn fast. Australia was *very* different. It seemed my overseas multi-lingual cross-cultural background was no longer of assistance. This was going to be a major intelligence operation. I would have to infiltrate the Organisation and discover its unwritten laws.

But my enquiries made me feel freakish. I stood there wanting to communicate, whereas Australians seemed perfectly happy just being, not wanting to say anything.

Added to that, nobody gave me any encouragement, nobody said, "You're doing fine, you're beginning to fit in nicely".

The problem was that I never knew whether or not I was surviving. Worse, I had no idea as to the minimum acclimatisation period before I'd be considered fit for the company of Australians. A month? A year? I asked around but nobody seemed to know. Most people growled — they seemed to hate the very idea of telling me anything.

After months of such lessons, of rejections and failed attempts, I began to get the point. To survive Australia, first and foremost I would have to adopt its customs. I would have to stand around for a while, if only to learn whether to grunt or say "thank you" when somebody brings you a beer.

I began to take notes . . .

For a start...
Don't ask questions

In Europe, in the States, even in turbulent South America, when you wish to find out something personal from someone you simply attract their attention, look them in the eyes and say:

"Now, what exactly was your father's mother's maiden name?"

The European will immediately launch into an elaborate family history of the past twenty generations. The Yank will recount all the hardships his paternal grandmother had to endure during her early years on the Missouri. South Americans will volunteer not only their grandmother's surname but her twelve other names as well, along with the names of all her famous lovers.

In Australia, ask the very same thing and you will be considered the rudest person on Earth. Asking questions is the one thing a true Australian never does.

By wanting to know something, you immediately become suspect. You are also labelled a "nuisance" because you are an effort to be with. It will also be considered that you are after personal gain.

Let's say you are having lunch with some new friends at the factory cafeteria or at the office where you have found employment. Excited and curious, you decide to get things going by making what you believe to be innocuous conversation*.

> YOU: What do you folks do on weekends?

> THEM: (An embarrassed silence and interchange of looks followed by an outbreak of mysterious unease)

*In Australia, there is no such thing as innocuous conversation.

9

Without knowing it, you have just made the following thoughtless allegations:

1 What gay bars do you frequent?

2 Don't your Alcoholics Anonymous meetings interfere with your weekend social life?

3 Do you happen to own a truck that could help me move my things on Sunday?

You are then likely to experience contorted mumbles due to mouthfuls of food, hurried excuses to leave the table, and glacial greetings for the next six months.

The Australian may want to know things, of course; curiosity is no less a human trait on the Lucky Isle than anywhere else. Australians may even be dying to find something out — but would certainly not dream of being so foolish as to allow natural instincts to take charge and permit the self-indulgence of actually asking.

What a successfully moulded Australian *would* say, when inquisitive, is:

"I understand from Jim Macleay that your grandmother was an Osborne girl."

To which the acquaintance will calmly answer: "No, no, you've got it wrong".

"Oh, I am sorry. I meant of course to say — a Chisholm."

"Wrong again", says the acquaintance with a twisted smile.

Confident that there are not more than two million names on any state's electoral list, resilient Australians will assume — quite correctly — that as long as they keep on trying, they must eventually get it right.

Of course, the alternative is not to ask anything in the first place — which is clearly what everyone has been doing all along.

This phobia about being asked questions remains to this moment a national trait which not even those practising it know about. Mention the topic to anyone and they will

Finding out information can be difficult

look away, as if you have suggested that Australians might hide a mystery or two in their backgrounds.

To be fair, however, it does not require too much to convince the average Australian that they are rather irritatingly sensitive to questions. They will accept what you say — then simply not talk to you for a long time. Eventually, they are likely to greet you one day with an aggressive:

"Why did you say that?"

To this sort of question, of course, a reply is not expected.

Overseas people ask questions because they want to know the answers. In Australia, you ask questions only when you don't.

Always seem busy

Australians are generally very keen to impart the feeling that they've just been interrupted at something really important. This way not only do they appear busy but they are able to force the other person to act apologetic and tense, thus helping to keep up the level of anxiety all around.

"Oh. It's you."

"I am sorry, I didn't realise you were busy."

"No, no. It's alright. I suppose."

"You did say I should feel free to call in."

"Yes . . . That was on Wednesday . . . Before this thing . . . But it doesn't matter . . . sort of."

It is of the essence to understand that Australians are fascinated by the concept of being busy. Being busy is a sign of success. Not being busy is also a sign of success, but we'll go into that later.

To produce the best possible impression, Australians usually employ the following conversation. Remember — no matter what two professionals *might* need to talk about, it is much more important to discuss how busy you have been.

"Sorry I haven't called you for a while but I've been flat out."

"Oh. I wouldn't've had time to talk to you anyway. It's been absolutely hectic."

"Anyway, I couldn't've even considered talking. Haven't been so busy in years."

"Even if you did find some time, I've been up to my

"It's absolutely frantic."

neck in work."

"How could I? I've hardly had time to breathe."

"Not as frantic as I."

"You're joking! I was completely snowed under."

"Well, I was going mad!"

"Crazy!"

"Hysterical!"

But being *too* busy could be interpreted as trying too hard. Worse even — as being pushy and wanting to rise above those around you. So just in case, it's best to be well-prepared and carry the following dialogue to whip out on occasions when you might be thought overly ambitious.

14

"In fact this is the first chance I've had to relax."
"Same here. No good working too hard."
"No point running yourself into the ground."
"Man's only got one life."
"Must take it easy."
"Too much work makes Jack a dull jerk."

The idea is to appear always tense (from being busy) but in a relaxed kind of way (from not being busy after all).

"I know just how you feel."

Never be interesting

Before arriving in Australia, I thought of myself as an average conversationalist. It came as a shock to discover that, in fact, I was an "interesting" person.

On hearing my views and opinions, which to me sounded rather ordinary, Australians would look up with astonishment and mutter:

"That's *very* interesting."

"Really?"

"Mmmm."

One day I ran into another LCT (Little Confused Tourist), who described an almost identical bewilderment. Likewise, it had been bothering him for a while.

"Do you find me fascinating?" he began.

"Not particularly."

"Just as I thought. Yet I am always told by everyone that what I have to say is fascinating."

"What an amazing coincidence!" I exclaimed. "People are just as rivetted by my own conversation!"

We took a long hard look at one another. Could it be that we were smarter than either of us thought?

"It does look like it, doesn't it?"

It was only after some deep soul-searching and several litres of coffee that we arrived at the truth.

1   People in Australia are deemed "interesting" when what they have to say is of absolutely no interest to anyone.

2   The moment views, aspirations or beliefs are considered to be "fascinating", it is best to switch the conversation to the weather.

Are you surviving Australia?

An acquaintance tells you some information you have never heard or thought about before. Pick the correct reaction from the three given below:

> (a) "That's interesting."

> (b) "I didn't realise that."

> (c) "Tell me some more."

The correct answer is — none of the above.

The Australian reaction would be, of course:

> "That can't be true."

This is the right response because you have limited life experience and you do not want anything or anyone to disturb it: you don't like conversations that stray too far away from accepted patterns.

And it shows that you know more than the other person anyway.

Greeting rituals

Australians, a happy-go-lucky and gregarious race of fatalists, are still somewhat confused as to what greetings to use in everyday encounters. "How do you do?" — too stuffy. "How are you?" — old fashioned. "Good day" is all right, but unless pronounced with perfect inflection* it does more harm than good. "Hello" is not too bad, but considered weak. "Hi" — short but too informal. "Ciao!" is only acceptable to those who know how to spell it.

For this reason, the best way to approach and greet people is to pretend that your mouth is full of hard-boiled eggs or, even better, to wait for someone to greet you first, and then echo their own favourite expressions.

"How are you?"
"How are you?"
"Nice to meet you."
"Nice to meet you."
"Enjoyed talking to you."
"Enjoyed talking to you too."

Tourists and Newcomers usually have to struggle through a gamut of greetings before they realise that the society which has produced the corked hat and the wide-toothed shearing comb has not as yet created a greeting acceptable to all.

Which brings us to that other point closely involved in the business of greeting — the problem of living in a classless society.

In Germany, a nation known for its sharp class

*Several comedians and politicians have risen to prominence, simply for knowing how to say "Good day" with the correct emphasis.

divisions, the greeting "Grüss Gott" is acceptable to everyone from accountant to count. Similarly, in France, birthplace of snobbery, two men exclaiming "Ca va?" know exactly what class they belong to, but are prepared to overlook it for the moment. In the Soviet Union "How do you bear yourself, Comrade?" can be used freely (even if only one of the two present is actually a bear).

It's only in Australia, the classless society, that people's egalitarian spirit won't allow them to come up with a greeting formula which could be uniformly used. This needs explaining.

The Australian jealously guards the privilege to be considered the equal of all. However, the idea is that it is *oneself* who is the equal, not necessarily the others. Thus the Australian cherishes the idea of walking up to the Queen or the Governor-General and being able to exclaim "G'day" — while becoming most upset should someone else actually do so. If the Queen herself said "G'day" to an Australian, there would be a revolution.

An Australian trying to be at ease

Putting Australians at ease

Asians never really feel at ease until they've been allowed to talk about their family and background. Mediterranean people like to be touched on the arms or hands in order to feel at home with you. Assuring them that they are the most sensitive and sentimental beings you've ever met, will relax Slavonic people just nicely.

So what relaxes an Australian? What puts Australians most at ease?

For one, letting them stand by the front door, hand on the door handle, with the security of being able to leave whenever they wish. Suddenly, they will become very talkative. Of course, this is the time to extract that vital information you've been dying to find out all night.

When inside your home, do not insist on getting Australians to sit down. They're much more likely to stay longer if they can stand up, lean against a doorpost, or sit on the edge of a table. You'll see how much friendlier they are this way, how much more they'll trust you and take you into their confidence.

Be as friendly as you like on the phone, as Australians do like a good disembodied, impersonal conversation. But when meeting the same person face to face later, be sure to act really stitched up. In fact, you will achieve far more if you just turn away and pretend that you are still on the phone to each other.

How to have nothing to say

For some time now, it has been realised that the greatest bar to peaceful co-existence in Australia are people who have something concrete to say. Factual statements and detailed descriptions are simply too dangerous, and those who sport them should be contained, as they're likely to cause trouble.

In the spirit of the industrious nineteenth-century British who created in their country a complex system of locks, weirs and canals in order to stem the course of unruly rivers, Australians have diligently perfected various methods of diverting, re-routing and flattening ideas and facts, which if left unattended could upset the natural balance of things.

For this reason, though books and editorials may occasionally be factual and informative, face to face communication ought to be uneasy, vague and full of abstractions.

A Serious Conversation

"It's harder than ever to get anywhere these days."
"Not as hard as it used to be."
"Maybe it's just a matter of finding one's niche."
"I don't think that applies any more."
"Most people get the short end of the stick."
"There's lots to be said for working from nine to five."
"It's still a question of priorities."
"Not if you cared about what you were doing."

An Everyday Conversation

"Not bad, eh!"
"Could've been worse."

> "My oath!"
> "Makes you think!"
> "You're not wrong there."
> "Might change but."
> "Pretty unlikely."
> "You never know."
> "Fair enough."

It's important to understand the principles that govern conversation in Australia. Not knowing them, you might make the mistake of trying to communicate.

In Australia you may say anything you wish, provided you do not back it up with facts. As most European-style conversation is too concrete and factual for Australian sensibilities, I take this opportunity to put forward some tried and true, evergreen conversational topics which are always likely to find favour with Australians.

1 Movies you missed on TV. Describe in meandering detail the circumstances that led you to come home late and catch only the last ten minutes of the movie under discussion. Lose interest once a person starts telling you the story.

2 Books. Never actually refer to books you've *read*, as that could lead to a difference of views. You're better off finding common ground with the other person by establishing what books both of you haven't read.

3 Winners you didn't back. This is an inexhaustible fount, as failure is a condition with which everyone can identify. Famous horses are the best. Lucky tips you've ignored just as good. In fact everything to do with horses except . . . winning.

4 Discussing or discovering common acquaintances could lead to serious blunders, so it's best to talk of people neither of you have ever met. Stars and politicians are

alright, but cookery experts are even better.

5 Talking of what you'd do if you won the lottery is very acceptable, since it permits both of you to rave on endlessly without having to listen to the other person.

6 Anybody can talk of the places they haven't been to as yet, but that promises to have no end in sight. It's best to talk of all the places you *wouldn't* want to visit. If you're from Sydney, mention Melbourne, or vice versa.

How not to say anything at all

Even the most minimal discussion of topics can land you in trouble. Best to limit yourself to expressions such as "I think it's too early to say". However, be careful not to appear as though you enjoy standing around, talking. Don't be afraid to walk out in the middle of a discussion, especially if you haven't yet said a word. It makes people uneasy, which is what Australians are used to.

Act inarticulate. Answer any questions put to you as if undergoing serious personal torment. Pull faces, scratch your ears, ruffle your hair, avoid direct replies and look positively offended at anything that might actually necessitate a reply.

If you must make a point, don't look at those you're talking to. Turn away, bend down, adjust your socks, play with your toes, glance under your armpits — anything in fact which might legitimately show that you're doing this under duress.

Above all, go by the Italian saying "In bocca chiusa, non entra mosca", meaning "Don't move your lips and the flies won't get in",* and practise in the bush in summer.

*Australians don't acknowledge foreign sayings, of course. Nevertheless Burke and Wills pointed out that the very first duty of good outback conversationalists is to keep their mouths shut.

Talking with your mouth closed so the flies won't get in

The Old Mate Style of greeting

Advanced greeting rituals

Australian friends, meeting by chance after not seeing each other for a variety of reasons, and for periods that could stretch from a few hours to thirty-five years, always go through an elaborate ritual that is not necessarily known for its coherence.

It is important to study this rite, as you may be called upon at a moment's notice to join in. For men, it will very likely take place in a public bar, i.e. in the presence of males only — all initiates of the ritual exchange.

The Inarticulate Style greeting is conducted in a low key by two friends of any age. Let us say that you are former members of the same football club and now encounter each other about three times a year. As usual, it is in a crowded hotel.

"How's it going, Tim?"

"Great. How's it going, Tony?"

"No complaints."

"That's good."

"Keeping fit?"

"Just fine. And you?"

"Fair enough."

"Anything new?"

"Anything new with you?"

"About the same."

"Same here."

"It's great to see you."

"Great to see you too."

The ritual ends when you part, saying, "See you later, Tim", and "See you around, Tony", or when someone suddenly breaks into actual conversation. Then there is no stopping Australians until they have replayed every football grand-final for the past ten years and checked through every racing bet they intend to lay that weekend.

The Old Mate Style greeting is extremely loud and involves much vigorous back-slapping and punching on arms and shoulders, as well as a fair bit of shadow boxing. Let us say that two mates, meeting at a car auction, haven't seen each other since the previous sale.

"Hide the babes in arms! Look who they've let out of the desert! It's Dingo!"

"Stone the crows! Bluey! You old codger! Fancy seeing you here!"

"Crikey! Fancy seeing you! Getting any, mate?"

"Climbing trees to get away from it! What about you? Getting any?"

"Got to swim under water to dodge it!"

"You look as if you couldn't crack hardy!"

"No worries, mate! I've been so busy, I had to put a man on!"

"Same old Bluey!"

"Same old Dingo!"

This ritual continues until one says, "Remember the time we . . ." Then the real talking starts and goes on forever.

The Itemised Style greeting is practised by two people full of concern for their respective families, who cannot think of anything else to say. For example, two clerks who haven't seen each other since they spent the annual holidays together (in a caravan park in Queensland), might go through the following:

"Hi, Barbara. How's Phil?"

"Hi, Rose. Phil's arm mended just fine. How's Mike?"

"Terrific, Barbara. He's managed to rebuild the whole van. What about little Trent, got over his mushroom poisoning?"

"No problems. Peter and Kerrie got over their diarrhoea, I hope?"

"Right as rain. What about Tom's bronchitis?"

"Hardly ever wheezes these days. And how is Daisy?"

"Hasn't bitten anyone since. And how was your Mum's operation?"

"Great. Open heart surgery really agrees with her. What about your Uncle Bill?"

"He's fine too. They're just about to give him back his licence. And your sister Beverley?"

"Oh, great. Still on crutches, but looking forward to next year's trip."

The dinner party

To be invited for dinner to a middle class Australian home is quite an honour. It is also a good idea to eat a decent meal beforehand.

The basic idea behind an Australian dinner party is to get together a group of men and women who are all used to eating at 6 pm, and then not feed them till well past nine.

To be fair, some bridging alimentation *is* provided about an hour after your arrival, in the shape of "savoury snacks". Make sure you are standing near the kitchen door as they are brought out, since the life span of these snacks, like those of invisible atomic particles created in laboratories, can only be measured in nanoseconds.

Before the actual dinner, you are expected to drink and join in the mixed conversation. "Mixed", of course, does not mean women with men. It's the topics and the drinks that are mixed. Clarice Thong, Duchess of Highborough, in her "Souvenirs Of An English Parasite's Wife", wrote of her visit to Australia in the early 1970s:

> *There is something terribly quaint about a country where men stand at one end of a room and women at the other. It's a very sensible way to behave given their condition, and Hewlett and I often wondered why it had not been made compulsory behaviour in other Third World countries as well.*

If forced into the position of having to make conversation with women, Australian males are usually careful not to say anything definite or concrete that might inadvertently reveal some secrets about themselves or their feelings. They prefer, instead, to gesticulate a great deal in graphic depiction of the "form" of things, rather than their "content". It is also customary to accompany all this arm-waving with a nervous laugh, in order to reassure "the ladies" that what is being said is not in the least important.

Australian females, on the other hand, prefer to take the stance of one left in charge of a large heap of rights and wrongs that desperately need sorting.

For this it's best to screw up your eyes and look slightly indisposed. Firmly clenched hands and a rigidly held body also help emphasise a point. The general aim is to stop the male in his tracks.

Lines of dialogue to be used for this purpose can be as follows:

"Oh, I don't think anyone would agree with that."

"How can you make such a statement!"

"You're being grossly unfair."

"That's a terrible generalisation."

After a few such exchanges, dinner may be served.

In China, a country with a three-thousand-year culinary history, dinner that does not consist of at least seven to ten dishes, is considered ill-mannered indeed. And this in times of famine. In Germany, home of the Large Portion, a plate that does not groan under vast quantities of food is simply not worth looking at.

By contrast, the Australian hostess, in her endeavour to be sophisticated, will spend a great deal of energy making sure that she has counted the right numbers of everything. You know, six guests — six t-bone steaks, six potatoes and three halved grilled tomatoes. After all, there is nothing better than simple, wholesome food.

"I'm sorry but someone here must have helped themselves to an extra potato."

"Oh, it must have been me."

"I'm afraid I'll have to ask for it back. Otherwise John misses out."

"John may have my portion too if he wishes."

"No, no, I want you to tell me what you think of it. I feel I may have overcooked it a bit."

Everybody knows that this is a trap. The Australian hostess, mother, wife, aunt or hotel proprietor just loves to run down her own cooking, to a point where it is downright difficult not to agree with her.

But, of course, you must never do this.

"I am sorry the cake's so dry."

"It's beautiful."

"I think I made it a bit too sweet."

"No! No! I love it!"

"I used all the right ingredients but added too much lemon."

"I can hardly taste it."

"But it's a lemon cake!"

"Oh."

"So you don't like it!"

No matter how cleverly you might be baited, hold steadfast to a contrary opinion. Whatever it is. Even if the food is tough as plastic, or drier than the mouths of Burke and Wills in the desert, you must insist that whatever you're eating is just perfect.

"Mmmmmm. That spoonful of gravy was superb."

"Thank you. I didn't make too much because I didn't want anyone to have to drown the natural taste of the meat."

"Ah, the meat! I've even eaten the grissle off the bone."

Just remember that you are expected to talk about the food. Endlessly. Australian guests know by instinct to praise everything placed before them, whether they like it or not. Having been trained at home over mother's cooking, they show their appreciation for every morsel they get.

The party

Since Australia represents a new society, new social laws apply. In the Olde Worlde style party, the rules of etiquette were set down rigidly. In the New World style party, there are no rules whatsoever. Everyone is free and spontaneous. However, several customs have inevitably developed over the years, and they are worth mentioning.

1 If you throw a party, under no circumstances are you to introduce guests to each other. The idea is to let people wander round aimlessly, feeling left out.

2 You must never have enough food to go round.

3 If you're a guest, and you brought along a bottle of scotch or champagne, make sure you point out to everyone what a fine label it is, but do not share it with anybody.

4 Ascertain that the house is furnished with wall to wall shag, then ash your cigarette on the carpet. On the other hand, if the party happens to be held outdoors, be careful to ash into someone's half-empty beer can.

5 Do not go around trying to express ideas or have an intelligent conversation. If you do end up in a huddle with someone, be careful

"... And he does have his romantic moments."

to talk only of things you know nothing about.*

6 Never invite an equal number of men and women. The aim is to keep up an artificial shortage so that after midnight, the boys can end up dancing with the boys.

7 Make sure that you leave the party so drunk that you can't remember where you parked the car. Walk about the suburbs till dawn, singing songs from beer commercials.

* There are several topics that must never be mentioned at parties: real feelings, true beliefs, actual voting habits, personal habits, any habits, history of mental illness, your income, your parents' income, the other person's income, and anything not in the the papers or on TV.

Never draw conclusions

Hiding in his Berlin bunker, Adolf Hitler saw that he was surrounded by Allied troops, concluded all was lost, declared the war closed and set fire to himself.

He wouldn't have done it had he been Australian. Australians, as a rule, are against drawing conclusions.

"Stone the crows! Bombs to the left, tanks to the right. Wonder if it's our boys. Maybe it's that other lot. Not much point worrying about it though. Reckon if I just keep mum a bit longer and stay down here in the bunker, things'll blow over."

Say you have moved into a small country town and it is your aim to integrate with the locals. Yours is the only CB radio in the street. Two days before Christmas, traditionally the stormiest time of the year, you hear on your set at 6.30 pm that flood waters have wiped out an entire area fifty kilometres to the north. It is your duty to tell everyone personally, then do nothing about it and turn up at the local pub for the rest of the evening.

But mere inactivity is no proof of your unwillingnes to draw conclusions. As a sign of your good faith, you should stand in the pub doorway as the waters rush towards you and express your bewilderment at the total suddenness of these things, and complain how December weather just isn't what it used to be.

There is constant pressure on the average Australian not to draw conclusions from events. You must show that you are straightforward, untainted by devious thought. You must be unable to predict anything more major than the third in the second at Randwick or Flemington on Wednesday.

"Relax, mate, it's only a summer shower."

Hence if it is likely that after the floods a cyclone will bear down, it would be most un-Australian to take any precautions other than tying up the dog.

Some time ago, I wrote a story about the experiences of a European doctor among Aboriginal tribes. One publisher perused my manuscript and shook his head.

"I am afraid this is not acceptable."

I looked sufficiently hurt to force an explanation.

"You predict here in your story that white Australians will be more and more willing to give back the Aborigines their rights as the Aborigines die out, no longer representing a danger due to their reduced numbers. I am afraid if we printed this, we'd be in hot water with everybody."

"It's how I view it."

"Oh come on, an Australian author's job is to describe things, not to add facts together and draw conclusions from them. It just isn't done. Where would that take contemporary literature? It's up to the readers, after all, to interpret it the way they want to."

Drawing conclusions, of course, is closely related to analysis. And analysis is another danger area that Australians don't get too close to.

A student — a young friend of mine who had recently arrived from Europe — achieved high marks in other subjects but failed her English exam. She took the offending essay back to her teacher, demanding an explanation for the low mark.

The teacher proved full of understanding.

"I've asked you here to analyse *Hamlet*. And so you go into long explanations of the characters' motives for their actions. And then you analyse Shakespeare's motives by pointing out his alternatives."

"Right. That's the way I learnt it in Europe", said the student.

"Well. In Australia, when you're asked to analyse a play like *Hamlet*, what we are really asking you to do is tell the story of *Hamlet*."

"Is that all? Why?"

"So we can be sure you've read the goddamn play!"

"But then why don't you just say 'describe *Hamlet*'?"

"Because 'describe' would mean 'give your opinion of it'!"

How to be moody

The Chinese will always greet you with the same degree of warmth. The Swiss, on the other hand, take a lot of trouble over their surliness, hoping that it will keep them neutral for another 800 years. A Brazilian would not dream of being anything but casual and friendly. In fact, in most places around the Globe, steadiness of temperament is held up to be a virtue.

Australians, however, being a freedom-loving people, do not believe in restricting themselves to such constant behaviour. Instead, as true sons and daughters of the great outdoors, they take their cue for personal relationships from . . . the weather.

In order to be in complete harmony with the elements, Australians have learnt to alter their moods rapidly and without prior warning. Having grown up in the unpredictable climate of the Fifth Continent, they feel that it is unnatural to be constant and that one ought to be suspicious of people who are.

I would advise all Tourists and Newcomers: abandon your old-fashioned constant ways and adopt moodiness as your new method of communication. This will not only repress more successfully those around you, but will also help instil a constant sense of guilt in everyone — a guilt which, being secret, is likely to cement Australian society even closer together.

Like the tropical cyclones that descend on this country out of the blue, moodiness is at its most effective when used for no apparent reason. There should never be any hint of an explanation. Never venture a motive for it.

"You look upset all of a sudden."

"It's nothing."

"Was it something I said?"

"I just realised that I've got to leave. I've got another appointment."

"But you said you had a free afternoon."

"Maybe I have. I'm not sure."

The aim of most moodiness, of course, is tension, tension and more tension. Yoga and other mystical fashions began to lose much of their popularity here when it was discovered that, with their emphasis on relaxation, they were cutting into people's moodiness and causing highly suspicious behaviour.

"You laughing at me or something, mate?"

"No, no, I am just beatifically happy."

"You were pretty happy this morning as well."

"It's this new inner peace I've found."

"Well, I better not find you laughing at me next time I see you."

In Latin America, archaeologists point with great pride at the achievements of the Aztecs and the Incas, who built great cities and palaces yet were ignorant of the wheel. In a like vein, Australian sociologists might show pride in the smooth running of Australian society, a society where constant good humour is all but unknown.

Moodiness is also used in the family, generally on young impressionable children *before* their ability for even temper has been developed.

"Hi, mum! I'm home!"

"Oh. It's you."

"Sure it's me. Wait till I show you this!"

"Not now. I'm in a Bad Mood."

"Later then?"

"Let's just hope you're a good boy and don't upset me."

By this method, the child quickly learns that not only has moodiness the ability to instil guilt in the moodee (that is, the person being mooded upon) but that anything new or interesting or different should be met with a repertory of moods that will, hopefully, prevent others from persisting with their ideas, or asking for your help.

Should someone come out with something like "Hello, Jim, I've been meaning to talk to you seriously", the silly, incoherent mood of neurotic giggles ought to be called into action. Suddenly everything is amusing. Wave your arms madly and try to stop the other person from saying anything important.

If this does not work, it is advisable to act as if you can hardly remember anything. For this purpose, look fierce of frown. Grimaces achieved by stretching lips and baring teeth are also effective. Scratching parts of the body is good, but not the crotch area as it is too Mediterranean.

If still not successful, try the blank mood. This is a distracted gaze, one that implies both toothache and a case of mistaken identity.

Last resort: the punch-up, the ultimate Australian mood. What "the blues" are to American blacks, "world-sorrow" to Romantic poets, or "satori" to Zen Buddhists, the punch-up is to Australians. Its unexpectedness and general baselessness make it endearingly antipodean.

How not to make requests

The Olde Worlde habit of coming straight out with a request is not going to be effective in a society that disapproves of questions. The Continental saying, "So shy she wouldn't ask the time of day", just does not apply to life in Australia. Here the less you ask for a thing directly, the more likely you are to get it.

It's best, therefore, to go around with a determined air of self-sufficiency, never letting anyone know what you are after. The very admission of a request puts the other person in an awkward position, i.e. they might have to do something about it.

Primitive and unsophisticated exchanges in places like Naples or Gdansk, based on the old question and answer formula, are over in a few short bursts:

"Why don't you ever take me out on your boat?"

"Haven't the time!"

"Won't you take me out just once for a few hours?"

"Alright! Alright! Tomorrow at seven?"

"Great!"

Contrast this with the profound exchange which Lucky Islanders have developed over many generations.

"Nice day."

"Yeah."

"I thought you'd be out on your boat."

"Too much trouble."

"I wonder what it would be like owning a boat."

"Oh. It's a lot of hassle."

"Yeah. I wouldn't mind buying one though."

"You should try mine."

"I'm not sure I'd have the time."

Australians abroad

"You'd love it. I might take you out tomorrow."

"I couldn't manage it earlier than seven."

"Right. Seven it is then."

"Oh, my car's in dock at the moment."

"Pick you up on the way."

"Great."

As you can see, an example of perfect understanding using neither question marks nor changes in intonation.

A note of caution. Make sure you don't get so used to these non-questioning habits that upon visiting Europe you take them with you. I am reminded of the sad story of a group of young Australians entombed in their Kombivan, circling around France desperately lost, but broadcasting loudly for all to hear: "She'll be right!"

How to make a cup of tea

For generations, the Japanese have been allowed to get away with the notion that theirs is the most advanced tea-making ceremony in the world. While no one disputes Japanese sophistication, it must be pointed out that the improvements wrought by Australians to the tea-making process have put this country in the forefront of the world's traditionalists.

Essential to the Australian tea ceremony is the concept of time. The Australian tea maker's aim is to put off the actual completion and serving of tea-proper for as long as possible.*

For this purpose, the Australian tea ritual begins long after the arrival of guests — especially if the guests were unexpected. In fact, its precise starting moment comes when the host begins to make vicious eyes at his wife, in response to which she reluctantly asks if anyone is thirsty.

"Tea would be nice", the parched guests mumble with swollen tongues.

Having finished her cigarette, the hostess jumps up, exclaims "Tea it is then!" and disappears into the kitchen, where she lights another cigarette.

After wiping down the sink, she fills the kettle to the very top with water, and re-emerges into the loungeroom, where she interrupts everybody by saying, "Water's on".

There's a stunned silence. The hostess puffs with

*Thereby, symbolically at least, delaying the twin processes of death and credit card repayments.

46

deep satisfaction, casting her husband murderous glances. (Legs on the coffee table, he reclines in complete immobility.) After the screeching of the kettle, she stubs out her cigarette and departs once more.

She looks for the sugar jar and picks out the hardened bits. She then puts some tea-leaves into the tea-pot but decides that tea-bags would be easier, so empties the unused tea-leaves into the sink.

Grabbing the carton of milk from the fridge, she carries it with the sugar bowl into the loungeroom, where she says, interrupting again, "Won't be long".

Back in the kitchen, she tries to match four cups and saucers, which she then transports into the loungeroom, saying, "Oh, I forgot the spoons".

Tea is now almost ready to be served. It is just that the water has to be re-boiled, as twenty minutes have elapsed since she switched off the kettle.

Keeping an eye on the water, she lights another cigarette. "Be with you in a sec!" she calls out to her guests as she finally pours the boiling water into the tea-pot.

Her entrance is greeted with gasps of delight.

"Ah, I'm looking forward to this!" says one.

"Nothing like a quick cuppa", says the other, without any irony at all.

Pleased, the hostess invites everyone to help themselves to tea, remarking with another murderous glance at the husband who still hasn't moved an inch:

"Sorry we don't have any biscuits, but Bruce ate them all last night."

Curbing your generosity

Everyone (in Europe, that is) knows that it is easier to be generous than mean. In generosity, one gives and forgets about it. Meanness, on the other hand, takes forethought, planning, organisation and a good deal of dodging.

Yet for all its straightforwardness, generosity in Australia is fraught with many dangers. A European friend of mine found this out after buying flowers, chocolates and other unimportant gifts for his Australian mates.

"You won't believe this", he exclaimed in agitation on one particular occasion, "but we went out last night, four of us blokes from the office, and we stayed out till past midnight. It was pleasant — everyone was nicely tense and unspontaneous — and we all enjoyed ourselves saying things we didn't mean and purely for effect, when right at the end I went and did a stupid thing."

"Don't tell me. You drank too much!"

"I probably didn't drink enough. One minute we were sitting around, punching each other on the shoulders, the next moment I was at the bar settling the whole account."

"Good God! You didn't!"

"I know! How the hell will I face my friends now? There will be this terribly embarrassing gulf between us, especially in lifts and at the staff canteen. They'll never invite me out in case I do it again."

"Well, would you like to go out with them again?"

"Yes, I would like to make sure that there are other such occasions. I won't do anything foolish. As it is, half the office refuses to talk to me because I've given them

When professional help is needed to curb your generosity

small gifts on the odd occasion."

"So why do you do it?"

"I don't know. They're only inexpensive items, but it seems to be enough to send people scampering down passageways and back into the lavatory when they see me coming."

"You've turned into the office creep!"

"Isn't it terrible? I'll have to seek professional help."

After extensive treatment, he was, he said one day, finally "cured".

"No more digging into my pockets before everyone else", he said with pride. "No more sneaking behind people's backs to settle restaurant accounts. Now I split the bill down to the last cent, and keep an eye out on whose turn it is to shout at the pub. I can even visit my friends without taking any presents, and if talk comes to money, I've learnt to change the topic quick smart in case anyone asks to borrow some."

"And are you happy?" I asked him.

"Very. But there is one problem. Now it's my ex-European friends who avoid me."

Never praise (unless it's expected)

A European wishing to praise someone, will throw his arms wide open, roll his eyes and declare in a loud voice: "You are undoubtedly the greatest, the most talented macaroni maker in Italy! You are not only a great craftsman but a gastronomical artist!"

Slightly exaggerated, to be sure, but on a continent of over five hundred million noisy souls, understandable. After all, how else is the message going to get through and make an impact? And then, perhaps the man *is* an artist, and why shouldn't he enjoy the appreciation of his craft?

In Australia, praise on such a lavish scale is not only unnecessary but positively dangerous. Australians would retort with comments like:

"What was all that about?"

"What's he *really* trying to say?"

"Is this a joke?"

"He must be drunk."

The Australian concept of praise runs in a different direction and as far away from absolutes as possible. In Australia, those wishing to show their appreciation will cautiously sum up the situation and then, after the necessary "errring" and "ummming", say in a quiet tone, something like:

"Not bad. Not bad, at all."

And if they *really* like it, they might even throw in a line such as "God, you must have been working hard" or, "I hope everyone appreciates the effort you put into this".

51

The aim is not only to avoid lavish praise but never to give unsolicited praise at all. In Australia, one may praise only if the other person has paved the way for it by rubbishing themselves first, with remarks like:

"I seem to have made a mess of things."

"I don't think I know what I am doing."

"It could have been better."

Of course, everyone understands that Australians, in running themselves down, are not really indulging in self-criticism but in fact giving the go-ahead to the other person for some medium-sized praise. The dialogue would run something like this:

"I don't know, this dress just doesn't fit me."
"Looks practically made for you."
"But I've chosen the wrong colour."
"I was about to say how well the colour suited you."
"It makes me appear too fat."
"You've never looked thinner."
"But I think I may have paid too much."
"No, no, you're so clever at finding bargains."

Take note. In the above type of situation, *not* praising could prove just as fatal as the offering at other times of unsolicited praise. For if you don't provide expected praise, Australians find themselves forced to take the last recourse and *praise themselves*.

"Hell, I don't know, I seem to have made a mess of things."
"Hmmm . . ."
"Even though I thought I was doing quite well."
"As a matter of fact . . ."
"Come on! It's not *that* bad!"
"I mean to say . . ."
"I happen to think that the whole thing is rather good, even if I say so myself."
"Errrr . . ."
"In fact, looking at it now, I would say it's excellent, bloody good, wonderful, terrific!"

Never criticise

"This is the worst piece of execrable rubbish I've ever had the misfortune to come across. You are not only clumsy, stupid and worthless, but you have the effrontery to waste my time as well as that of the rest of Europe."

In Germany, you could be considered a fool, should you come up with anything less critical.

Don't try it in Australia.

In France, such a mild approach to the mistakes of others would not even rate a mention. The French, who take their critical faculties seriously, would closely examine the offending object. They are then likely to give a comprehensive list of those who have attempted it far more successfully but are still considered second-raters. This would follow with a list of all those who have done it well. It is highly likely they will then take the offending object, item, piece, etc., and throw it to the ground, spitting copiously, trampling it underfoot, and vowing to kill anyone who might ever again present them with such *merde*.

Don't try it in Australia.

In the United States, criticism is taken very seriously indeed. The American, who holds nothing more sacred than the concept of "progress", will come out with something like:

"Now look here, buddy boy, I don't care who and what you are, but you can't come up with stuff like this. What you'll really have to do is follow my advice, since I am much better, bigger, brighter and wiser than you!"

Don't try it in Australia.

When I first found myself in this country, I gained information about the place from movies, plays and television dramas. They displayed Australians as a forthright people who are forever involved in gutsy arguments, violent verbal skirmishes and fearless face-to-face confrontations; neither afraid to openly speak their minds nor resentful when others do so.

Nothing could be further from the truth.

Australians do not believe in the rights of others to be critical of their efforts at all. A Lucky Islander may be self-critical, true, but that is merely being Low Key, not unlike those Chinese Mandarins who used to refer to everything they owned or did as "humble".

This basic rule leapt at me the following way. An Australian friend, proud of his newly built outdoor barbecue, kept urging me for weeks on end to tell him what I thought of his handiwork. For weeks on end I assured him that it was very, very good. But no matter how much I insisted, he always closed the discussion with the remark: "Ah, it still needs a bit of work".

One day, as talk drifted onto the subject of his barbecue again, I decided to give in by agreeing with his own evaluation. So when he finally popped the question "What do you really think of it?", I told him, "Well, I imagine it stills needs a bit of work".

There was a painful and embarrassed silence. My friend simply sat there, and said nothing for a long, long time. After that I never heard from him again.

Criticism is the one thing Australians are simply not prepared for. They may request it. They may even tell you that they crave it. But you must never ever give in to the temptation. No matter how hard your friends, superiors or employees try to get an "honest" opinion out of you, no matter how earnestly you are assured that it is alright, that you can really speak your mind — don't soften. Don't give in. Hold to your initial opinion that everything is just perfect.

Say your friend has just brought around the plans for her new loungeroom, and she wants your honest thoughts on the subject.

"I'm so glad you like it!"

You know better than to comment on how the chequered wallpaper clashes with the patterned carpet, or on the blue curtains with the salmon lounge-suite, or on the idea of having a glass coffee-table surrounded by fake rococco armchairs.

"It will look very nice", you remark enthusiastically.

But still she insists: "No, no, tell me the truth. If there is something you don't like, it can easily be changed".

(Hey, how do you change *everything?*)

"I tell you, it's wonderful what you've planned."

"But no, I want you to really tell me."

Finally you break down and say: "I think the Chinese rosewood sideboard doesn't quite fit in —"

"But can't you see?" exclaims your friend, outraged. "The pink in the wood will be reflected in the wallpaper! I've always decorated my own places. What's more, everyone's always been very positive! I really didn't expect you to be so small-minded. I'd never say something like that to you. Anyway, I worked for what I've got and I can do what I like. I have to leave now. I am going out."

In Australia, NEVER EVER CRITICISE. There are only two standard responses to criticism:

1 They'll take years to forgive you, or

2 You'll never hear from them again.

The problem with offering criticism in Australia lies in the fact that before you have finished speaking, people are ready with a levelling explanation of why things are the way they are — thus making whatever you say both irrelevant and insulting.

Helping out one's mates

As inheritors in the main of an Anglo-Saxon culture, Australians have a deep respect for the democratic ways of life. This means that they feel no sympathy for the money grabbing, avaricious and unpleasant habits prevalent in other countries.

Take, for instance, corruption.

When an Italian pays off a Mafia member to get his son off military service, it is, undoubtedly, bribery. When a Russian gives a large sum of money to a Party official to get him a car ahead of 100,000 others, that too is called bribery. When an Australian slips some money to someone to get his brother off a drink-driving charge, he is not bribing anybody. He is simply making a donation.

Straight out bribery is a foreign habit, practised by grubby, self-motivated people with slicked-back hair and hirsute fingers, who live in faraway lands. Donations, no matter to what obscure causes, are sunny, kind, charitable and typically Australian.

Naturally, an Australian in trouble will want to find the way out of it as much as any Peruvian or Frenchman. It also goes without saying that there are ways of attenuating one's woes — but never at the expense of jeopardising one thousand years of built-in, Anglo-Saxon respect for the law.

That is why an Australian may "help out a mate", he* may "do someone a favour", he may even "push another's cause", and if it is "made worth his while", he might even "stick his neck out for you", or "bend the

*Women appear to be precluded from the use of the word "mate".

57

Helping out one's mates

rules a little". He knows that what he is doing could never possibly be called corruption.

After all, "corrupt" countries are run by greasy dictators aided by fat officials in shiny suits and with heavy accents, who take the whole thing very seriously — in a style far removed from the light-hearted, matey, easy going Australian way.

So what you must do, in trying to extricate yourself from trouble, is look around for someone who'll give you a knowing wink and an understanding response like:

"I've got a mate who might be able to help you."

"I know this great bloke who's never let down a mate yet."

"What you want is a little mate with the right connections."

This is the cue. The moment a mate, or a mate's capacity, is mentioned, you know that you are on the right track. Chances of clambering out of trouble have now greatly increased, and you should welcome the other person's offer with laughing snorts and some light-hearted frivolity.

"D'you reckon he'll want to help a geezer like me? Heh! Heh! Heh!"

"Ah, well, you might have to make it worth his while. After all, he's got to come in from Vaucluse! Hah! Hah! Hah!"

A slightly derisory and jovial attitude is necessary as proof that this is neither corruption nor an illegal connivance, but really a kindly turn, a friendly game between mates, who are basically superior to any dirty and deliberate breaking of the law.

How to react to the police

You have to exhibit a certain amount of fear. Police become very suspicious of people who do not show some anxiety. Even police get anxious when they run into other police.

It's advisable to act tense to prove that you are innocent. All the guilty people, who have much more time to watch phoney TV police shows, tend to act really relaxed. The way to achieve the tense look is to tell yourself, the moment you see a blue uniform:

"Ah, there's the police. I must be doing something wrong."

If you happen to come from a Continental type environment where a healthy disregard for the law has been the practice for the past few hundred years, then the best way to inspire fear in yourself at the sight of the police is to think thoughts such as:

"Maybe paying $75 for that new 26-inch stereo TV *was* a bit cheap . . ."

"I wonder if the bond money on that old flat *did* cover the last four weeks' rent?"

Though this system is partially effective, it still cannot bring police and the general public closer together. Unfortunately, the only people in Australia who understand the police are the criminals. But that's only natural since they spend so much time together.

Even police are scared of police . . .

Hints for the young

1 If you are a nice little girl or boy, you should never talk to anyone in the street, even if they are your grandparents. It's best if you ignore them or set the dog on them. Until you are at least 55 years old and too ancient to be of interest to anyone, you will not be able to judge whether a person is trustworthy or not.

2 Never hold your Dad's hand for more than a couple of seconds, and even then make sure you follow it with a quick jab in the stomach. If you find that your Dad does show more feeling for you than natural (i.e. never), make sure you tell your Mum about it and she'll stick up for you.

3 Never touch your friends. What will people think?

4 Physical affection can also lead to evils like emotional dependence. Your Mummy and Daddy, who know best from experience, will be able to tell you that those who like people, get hurt! If you have to put your arm around something, it's best to put it around a beer bottle.

How to make an Australian sandwich

In Germany, if you wish for a quick snack, someone is sure to fix one up within minutes of your asking. With Teutonic precision, German sandwich-makers will butter a dozen slices of pumpernickel, fill them with Berliner and Bismarck herrings which are always kept in the fridge at the ready, and cut them neatly into halves. It's a fast and uninterrupted blitz.

Naturally in Australia such precision is frowned upon. Australians, a nation of individualists, like to give their sandwich-making that personal touch. Therefore preparing a snack becomes not so much a chore as an expression of the snack-maker's inner thermos. Rather, ethos.

Once you too have decided to be an individualist, you're ready to make an Australian sandwich. Once you've mastered this, improvisation and mayonnaise may freely flow. Here then are the basic steps to follow.

Remove Tip Top from Westinghouse. Take two to six slices out, keep them in hand, and wander around kitchen trying to locate a Noritake plate. Place slices on edge of stove to answer the telephone. Back in kitchen, remember tin of Golden Circle stored in corner of colonial-style smooth edge cupboard. Place Golden Circle on top of TV Week.

Pick up bread from edge of stove and rummage for Staysharp knife behind stack of Tupperware. Spread Norco on bread. Light a cigarette. Catch glimpse of interesting article in TV Week lying on table. Take Golden Circle from top of magazine stack and place on edge of stove, buttered slices on Knebel bench, unbuttered ones on K-tel Kitchenmate, loaf of Tip Top back into Westinghouse, Staysharp on table. Finish reading TV Week.

Transfer buttered slices from bench to table. Move stack of Women's Weeklies and old TV Weeks to sideboard to make room. Transfer boiled eggs from fridge to edge of sink. Notice patchily buttered slices and spread Norco to same evenness throughout. Transfer Staysharp to bench.

Take plate off table and move it closer to buttered slices on bench. Locate last Vegemite jar behind tins of Pal. Hold Vegemite under hot water to loosen lid. Look around for Staysharp to prize lid open. Transfer magazines from sideboard to sink, convinced that knife has fallen behind them. (In fact it's under the plate on the bench.)

Mix Lea & Perrins curry powder. Look for eggs. Salvage from under stack of Women's Weeklies on edge of sink. Attempt to light another cigarette. Replace flint in Dunhill lighter. Move buttered bread, Vegemite, squashed eggs and Golden Circle to table. TV Weeks back to sideboard, Staysharp into sink.

Sit down exhausted. Get up again. Put teaspoon of Nescafe into cup, add sugar and Longlife milk. Put into Toshiba microwave, sit down again, and watch the boiling coffee turning slowly around.

You're now ready to make that sandwich.

How to be Low Key

Quintessentially *the* Aussie trait — especially when dealing with people.

Being Low Key is neither a mannerism nor a fashion. It is as basic to being Australian as rust is to motor cars, or grey fur to koalas.

Low Key has to do with pretending that you're a lot less than what others think you are (if this is possible).

Being Low Key also means wearing unfashionable clothes (see next topic). Remember at all times that the actual quality of the clothes in your wardrobe is not important. What really matters is that they should look as if they were meant for somebody else.

Low Key has to do with being awkward, clumsy and rather ungrammatical.

Achievements, assets, attitudes, should only be referred to with badly constructed ... you know ... lots of punctuation marks ... sort of ... obliquely ... and how can one put it ... Uncertain ...?

Ambition must also be heavily played down and its hard-earned fruits should always be attributed to ... err ... Luck?

Low Keyness doesn't only mean being unable to formulate sentences about your own successes. It also means cutting off other people as they are trying to tell you something successful about themselves.

Low Key has to do with warding off envy.

Like the plumber who has just won a tray of meat at a pub raffle. He knows how to be Low Key, by instinct. And his mates, holders of the losing tickets, surround him with a twinge of envy, as he keeps fumbling with his prize.

PLUMBER: Yeah . . . yeah . . . yeah . . .
MATES: A tray of meat, eh?
PLUMBER: (Laughs nervously) Heh! Heh! Heh!
MATES: Last week it was turkey!
PLUMBER: (Sadly) But I like turkey.
(Nice uneasy atmosphere but at least nobody's resentful.)

Being Low Key also puts a nice reassuring gulf between yourself and those who might want to get close.
Like women.
Opening doors for the opposite sex is fine but make sure you get in the way as she is trying to pass you. Rush to offer her a lighter *after* she's already fished out her own. Farting in bed is OK too, but make sure you first let out an enthusiastic "Wait for it!".

Antipodean chivalry

66

How not
to dress well

Overseas, people's clothes indicate the social class they come from. In Australia, clothes are meant to disguise it.

This transcendental truth came to me early on and quite by accident. I was taken along to the home of a wealthy land developer where, I was assured, I would meet rich and important people. I went to seek out my host and addressed the most elegant man present. It turned out he was the maitre d'. The second most elegant man turned out to be the pianist hired for the evening. The third best dressed man was someone's bodyguard. My search continued down the line, until finally I found my host: he was wearing the crumpled suit and battered shoes of a man who's come to give a quote on removing the vermin.

I expressed my astonishment, since back in Europe a rich man would rather kill himself than be seen in such an outfit. In Europe, elegance is an obsession. The concept of "everything he owns, he wears on his back" was devised to designate a large percentage of the continent's population. Europeans who don't look more than they are worth, get a raw deal indeed, and stories about such people are legion.

"The richer one is in Australia," explained my host, "the poorer he must dress, in order to keep the nation democratic. I know this may seem difficult to understand since Australia is such a free and affluent country, but you could visualise it in terms of being an escapee from Siberia, trying to make your way across the Soviet Union to the Norwegian border. At all costs, you would

Dressing down for the occasion

The best of both worlds

want to blend in with the environment, and wherever possible, disappear from view completely."

"So what is one escaping from in Australia?" I asked.

"Envy."

It was my first lesson in being Low Key.

Not long ago, I happened to be talking to a factory owner, when a flashily dressed young man rushed past his employer. As the young worker disappeared in his gleaming sportscar, the factory owner remarked:

"I wish I could afford his style."

To the casual listener, the statement might have been a reflection on the man's financial affairs. As a matter of fact, they were rather healthy. What he was referring to, of course, was the fact that as a successful capitalist, he simply could not "afford" to be seen as such. He should not be seen in anything less Low Key than an off-the-rack, ill-fitting, dull grey suit.

In short, in Europe when people dress poorly, they do so for one reason — poverty. In Australia, where one pays a great deal of attention to not being paid attention, poor dress is the aim.

First of all, when shopping for clothes, you must

ascertain a poor fit. Features to look for are trousers that are slightly too short (as if they had shrunk on the buyer), of a material that crushes easily. Jackets must be a few years behind the fashion. Any fashion. If very narrow lapels are the vogue, then choose medium or wide. If wide lapels are the rage, choose medium or narrow. Real difficulties arise only when medium lapels come into fashion. As with all problematic choices in Australia, one suspects that the solution lies somewhere in alcohol.

Of footwear not more than two pairs are needed: brown shoes to go with blue, black or grey trousers, and black shoes to go with brown, fawn or white. The theme of this colour scheme should be carried right through the entire wardrobe.

In the "casual" footwear department, thongs can be worn with everything.

The Australian woman has a lot more freedom because her choice of mis-matchable colours is so much broader.

The first stop of a woman shopping for clothes should be at the synthetics counter of a department store. This is where you will find the backbone of your summer or winter collection.

You need no more than six dresses, as Sundays may be spent in any brushed nylon brunch-coat. None of the dresses should be tainted by fashion or style. Go for the shirt-maker or cowl-neckline, as they always bunch up under a cardigan and look suitably gauche.

Blouses must be in a variety of prints so that they may be mis-matched in the highest number of permutations, while at the same time allowing you to look like everyone else.

Shoes and handbags need not be bought with any specific outfit in mind, as they can thus be grabbed at random from the pile at the bottom of the cupboard. The only requisite is that the shoes should at least match with . . . each other.

Why artists look like accountants

In Europe, successful artists are usually known for their colourful personalities. There was once a famous European playwright who lived well beyond his means. Every day, his creditors would clamour outside his door, demanding payment. To satisfy them, the playwright would once a year put the names of all his creditors in a hat, and draw out ten of them; only these ten would then get paid.

One particularly unlucky tradesman's name had failed to come up year after year. He became hysterical. "Sir!" he shouted. "If you cannot afford it, you shouldn't live in such luxury! I will cause a scandal!" The playwright, however, warned him with a stern voice: "Keep quiet, sir, or next time I won't even put your name in the hat!"

It couldn't happen in Australia.

Far from being extravagant and colourful, successful artists in Australia take pride in their frugality and ordinariness. My first encounter with one of the species was at a party.

"And who is that quiet little accountant in the corner?" I asked rather loudly of my hostess, finding out only too late that I had probably made an enemy for life of a well-known serious composer.

But to my surprise, I saw a slick of satisfaction spread across the man's face. Unknowingly, I had paid him a compliment. Later, I found out that the poor man had always felt that people did not consider him to be making an honest living. He therefore tried to seem as ordinary and as average as possible.

Women prefer to run the arts

Very soon I learnt that Australians feel much more at ease with artists who not only have the appearance of accountants, but their regular habits as well. Rising early is *de rigueur,* eating toast with Vegemite a must; wearing terry-towelling hats to the footy or the cricket is essential.

For this reason, most successful people in the arts are careful to let it be known that being a creative person in Australia is really a nine-to-five job. They insist that these hours are the most inspirational, and that creating outside them is rather unprofessional. This relaxes everybody and reassures them that what artists are doing is in truth good, old-fashioned, hard sweat-of-the-brow type work.

Musicians like Mozart and Handel, or writers like Balzac and Dickens, working around the clock, managed to knock up whole operas or novels in a matter of days. They were guilty of amateurish and unprofessional methods simply not tolerated on the serious Australian creative scene. Not only were these artists too fast and unmindful of unionist work ethics, but to make matters worse, not one of them was ever known to mow his lawn, change the wheel of a carriage or belong to a baby-sitter club.

State-of-the-art survival

Should you decide to become a purveyor of the Arts, it would be in your better interests to follow the basic rules that make entertainment in Australia both unique and peculiarly antipodean. Here are some suggestions.

1 Classical Drama

When presenting a classical play, you must change it beyond recognition, so as to cause the audience to wonder why on earth the work became famous in the first place. You must also call this new mess an "up-dated adaptation". It is quite acceptable to treat the author and the public as morons.

2 Classical Music

If possible, never tune a piano correctly for either concerts or recitals, in order to be able to test the musical sensibilities of the audience to the fullest. Also, overseas soloists should be instructed that the real purpose of applause in Australia is not to show appreciation but to see, as a matter of principle, just how many encores may be squeezed out of a jet-lagged and otherwise exhausted performer.

3 The Australian Film Industry

Every few decades, Australians like to get together and decide to have a film industry. To the credit of the indomitable Australian spirit, film makers in this country just don't know when to give up.

This is necessary as all previous Australian efforts to make internationally successful films have had to be

It's not a love story!
It's not erotic!
Minimum of relationships!
Nice photography
Authentic Costumes!

PICNIC AT GALLIPOLI

abandoned. The following are generally to blame: American distributors, greedy unions, the poms, the brain drain, lack of talent, small budgets, big budgets, too many films, not enough films, poor scripts, too many producers, unscrupulous investors, public apathy, interference, rising wages and the falling dollar.

Currently the industry is being helped along by a sudden upsurge in script writers. Whereas before the war it was fashionable to write poems, nowadays it is the fashion to write film scripts. This is an excellent cure for broken hearts or those recovering from a shattering divorce. But no matter how therapeutic writing a film script may be, you must try to please Australian producers and distributors.

To start with, your scenario ought to have the following basic ingredients:

(a) a hero who suffers from unspoken resentments, gets into trouble with the authorities, and has never read a book in his life;

(b) a heroine who cannot cook, is not too pretty, and has sex no more than twice a year.

Should the film be set in some exotic location like the Far East or Turkey, it is vital that the hero never falls in love with or even gets close to one of the locals. It is best if he doesn't fall in love with anyone at all, unless it be with a rusting motor car at the back of a paddock.

His company must be strictly expatriate Anglo-Saxon comprised of men to whom he is obviously superior, but who are the only ones able to supply him with the monosyllabic conversation he needs with his beer.

Should the film be a costume drama set in some earlier period of Australian history, make sure you present a picture of the past which is both historically unlikely and flattering. No mention must be made of excruciating poverty, chronic loneliness, pathetic alcoholism or rampant homosexuality.

Instead, you ought to present characters in immaculately tailored period costumes, living in stylishly colour-coordinated homes. They must never swear or sport disgusting personal habits.

With films that take place in contemporary Australia, matters are rather more straightforward. The society that you describe should be homogenous, 100% Anglo-Saxon (with a dash of Celtic to keep grandpa happy) — and your heroes should bear names like Terry, Duncan and Bruce.

4 Art Galleries
Art galleries should, as a rule, be situated in narrow, inaccessible lanes or built along busy clearways, a half hour's walk from the nearest parking. It is advisable to employ assistants who can make clients feel inferior and stupid. If such are unavailable, hire a pretty teenage boy.

The grant system, or How to buy a block of flats

The fundamental way to survive the Arts in Australia is to understand the Grant System. It is designed to appeal to the innate gambling spirit of all Australians. Those who apply for grants understand intrinsically that their application is not much different from having a flutter on the horses or dogs.

But as the popular Australian saying goes, "You've got to be in it to win it". Therefore every month of an artist's year should represent the closing date of a particular government grant.

JANUARY   Special Purpose Grant
(Deceased Estate Auction: down payment on neglected three-storey block of flats)

FEBRUARY   Senior Fellowship Grant
(legal costs and stamp duty)

MARCH   Creative Development Grant
(new guttering and plumbing and a new section of roof)

APRIL   Script Assistance Grant
(re-carpeting of three-storey stairwell)

MAY   Overseas Research Grant
(light fittings and chandeliers to be bought in Hong Kong)

JUNE	Second Reassessment Grant (pay accountant and sundries)
JULY	Federal Arts Award Grant (garbage disposal unit)
AUGUST	Multicultural Studies Grant (Italian marble for the hallway)
SEPTEMBER	Special Projects Grant (repair built-ins and furniture)
OCTOBER	Visual Arts Exchange Fellowship (repaint walls and make good)
NOVEMBER	Special Environmental Studies Grant (landscape back and front gardens)
DECEMBER	Overseas Study Tour Grant (down payment on the block of flats next door, then off on long deserved holiday)

When filling in grant forms, your stated aims must sound determined, idealistic and non-controversial. It would be helpful if you could prove that the project has already been successfully done overseas.

During the interview, you should appear relaxed, non-ambitious and friendly — in a frigid sort of a way, of course. If interviewers act too friendly you can be sure you missed out. It helps to have had an affair with one of the assessors first.

Once you have the money, immediately ask for a hefty extension of one or two years, "due to other commitments". Divorce is a good excuse for women. Having to look after the kids is the usual excuse for men.

After several such extensions, publish in a Saturday morning paper your reasons for not fulfilling your obligations to date, followed up by an attack on the whole Grant System. Then apply for a grant to research the state of the Arts in Australia, on the basis of your two-part newspaper article (second part of which, still incomplete).

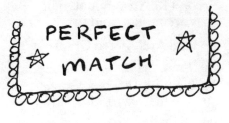

Underdog and hotdog

Getting on top of the Underdog

Australians are notorious for their sympathy with the Underdog. Far from being a mere figure of speech, the Underdog is as vital to modern day legends as the hero Siegfried was to Norse mythology. In fact, should anyone even so much as hint in passing at the word "Underdog", you must immediately chip in:

"Oh, I don't know, but I have this gut reaction to be on the side of the Underdog."

It's important to say this, because right away it will identify you as a person who:

1   Is not likely to rock the boat (only taking the side of a Tall Poppy would do that);

2   Is likely to lend money should the other person ask for it; and

3   Has no idea what they are talking about.

It also takes quite some time to realise that while you must always claim to take the side of the Underdog, you should never admit to being one. Do not be tempted to tell your audience, in the middle of a story:

"It was terrible — there we were fighting outside the pub, with a big crowd around us, and I was the Underdog."

Underdogginess, like being mauled by sharks, clearly happens only to other people.

How to survive a Fair Go

While the French produced the baffling ideas of Existentialism and the Germans discovered the potent laws of Dialectics, Australians were also busy, giving the world the complex concept of the Fair Go.

No other theory encapsulates so successfully the general Australian outlook on life, which decrees that anything good, worthwhile or pleasant, cannot possibly last.

The concept of a Fair Go is about letting people make fools of themselves. It is about enjoying other people's mistakes.

For example, if some friends happen to start a small business and their initial efforts meet with success, it is only fair that you should warn them against every possible disaster lurking around the corner, then leave them completely on their own.

This, you must point out, should not depress them as by the unwritten laws of a Fair Go, though the business might go bankrupt, they can always start again.

Also, by the same rule, should any friends speak of a scheme to make them rich or famous, it becomes your duty to protect them from the dangers of their own personal ambitions. Philosophical arguments to be used on such occasions are:

"It's already been done."

"The multinationals will get you."

"It's the worst possible time to do it."

"I know someone who tried and today they're being

It pays to be self-sufficient

looked after by the Salvation Army."

Conversely, if you have any worthwhile plans yourself, you ought to keep them as secret as possible — especially from your friends.

How to recognise a Tall Poppy

The ancient Greeks used to say that before the gods destroyed a man, they gave him everything. In a like vein, "Tall Poppy" is the designation Australians give their more successful enemies, just before attempting to destroy them.

You will hear a lot about Tall Poppies. All sorts of people will tell you that Tall Poppies, on the whole, are disliked, and that people turn against those who rise too high above others. Of course, being "poppies" they can only be a bit taller than the rest in the field. This is some comfort, perhaps, but of no consequence whatsoever to the "great Australian levellers".*

You mustn't, however, expect to meet anyone who actually admits to a personal dislike of Tall Poppies. By a strange quirk of circumstances, it seems that it is always the "jealous masses" who dislike Tall Poppies, never the speakers themselves.

As no one has ever come out publicly against Tall Poppies, their general characteristics can only be guessed at. Here are a few I have managed to ascertain:

1 Tall Poppies are just like you and me only more so.

2 They're usually below average height. This reputedly drives them harder.

These "levellers" are not responsible for the flat topography of the country as many Newcomers erroneously suppose.

A Tall Poppy Squad at work

3 They never live overseas. If they did they would be known instead as Successes — providing, of course, that they still call Australia "home".

Never question
ancestry

In some Eastern European countries, every couple of years the Government issues a new textbook in which all past events have been thoroughly altered to suit the ruling dictator's immediate political needs. This not only helps the country's leader hang on to his job, but saves the trouble of having to interpret the present in terms of the past, as the past has obligingly adapted itself to suit the present.

By contrast, the history of Australia is a very simple affair. The truth can be neither altered nor denied. It is so widely known that a newcomer to this country need not even read the actual books. Just by talking to people, you can pick up all the historical background you need to know.

It is common knowledge, for instance, that the condemned convicts on that First Fleet were vastly outnumbered by the hundreds of officers sent over to guard them. This ratio discrepancy can easily be verified even now, two hundred years later, simply by talking to the huge number of families who can trace their lineage back to the officers of the First Fleet.

It is also commonly known that the country's early settlers, even if sent over as convicts, were generally guilty of crimes no worse than stealing a loaf of bread or a leg of ham, crimes which, owing to the harshness of the British judicial system of the times, were enough to have them most unfairly exiled to the Southern Hemisphere for life.

By a strange quirk of nature, those few convicts who *were* indeed guilty of heinous crimes and ended up on

"...The better known side of the family."

the shores of Botany Bay, proved to be either sterile or homosexual. This fortunate correspondence between criminality and incapacity to produce offspring was one of the future nation's lucky breaks. It saved countless generations from having to come to terms with any unpleasantness in their background.

Though there was a fair amount of interchange between early settlers and the local Aborigines, the relationship seems to have remained on a platonic level, with the two sides being more involved in deciding whether suburbs would bear English or native names, rather than in setting the common foundation of a new race of people. This is evidently why during the last two hundred years of Australian history, no prominent personality, political or artistic, has ever come forward and admitted to any Aboriginal ancestry — unless they were Aboriginal, of course.

Later another stroke of luck befell the future nation. Waves of young aristocrats descended upon the colony. Eccentric third and fourth sons of British earls and baronets, they came over for the sole purpose, it would seem, of sireing a host of middle-class families with double-barrelled names.

The descendants of these enthusiastic youngbloods are usually reticent beings who do not like to bring to light their elevated lineage. Instead they spend their time hiding from public glare (i.e. embarrassing questions) in clubs and associations designed to remind everyone of English upper class conditions of 150 years ago.

Why losers
are heroes

When the English lose at competitive sports, the loss is attributed to bad luck. If an American loses, people blame inadequate training. When an Australian loses, no blame is attached at all. On the contrary, the event is regarded as a special achievement and the sportsman or sportswoman is praised for:

(a) trying very hard

(b) having given their all

(c) making 14th when they could have come last.

Besides glory and public recognition, the loser with enough failures to their credit also receives that highest accolade. of all — becoming a universally recognised Little Aussie Battler. What gladiators were to the Romans, or kamikazes to the Japanese, Little Aussie Battlers are to the folks of the Fifth Continent. They are the legendary heroes and heroines who fight against all odds . . . and lose.

Spectators in a European or South American stadium will berate and curse their favourite team for the slightest mistake. Threatening the umpire with disembowelment is a must. Running onto the field with a machete is also quite popular. Declaring war on the rival team's country is a further variation.

One should not expect any of this in Australia.

While in other parts of the world a sports fan may come away from a lost match scarlet with rage, veins popping, only this side of a stroke, in Australia you must

"It's bronze, bronze, bronze for Australia! And the gold and silver went to — er, let me see . . ."

walk away from even the greatest disaster only ever so slightly sad. Calling your favourite bested player or team "great", "brave", "wonderful", or just plain "terrific" — humiliation after humiliation — is highly recommended. No compliment should ever be good enough.

A certain fascination for failure is a requisite of living in Australia. In simpler terms, while overseas people look forward to success, in Australia it is failure that's the source of greatest joy. If talking of friends, mention only those who lost all their money. If discussion touches on history, quote only lost battles, preferably by Australian or British troops. It's important to understand that whereas even kindergarten children can give you a list of battles lost by the "good guys" (Eureka, Gallipoli, etc.), most graduates find it hard to name a single battle where Australians have triumphed.

Australians have long accepted that there is something trustworthy about failure. Ned Kelly failed and he's revered for it. If only Howard Florey had just missed out on discovering penicillin — instead of actually discovering it — he could have had shopping centres named after him.

After all, if you win, nobody knows whether you're really doing your best. It might have simply been luck. If you come second, or third, or even last, people at least will know that you've exerted yourself. Then there is the added knowledge that if you've won, you've probably cheated, or tried too hard, at the expense of something in your personal life.

Whereas if you lose, at least you're honest.

Cricket

The Americans do not have to play cricket because they beat the English, fair and square, in the 1776 War of Independence.

Australians, who have not as yet had the chance to get stuck into the English in open warfare, hang on to cricket, hoping thus to prove themselves the better and the stronger.

Cricket is essentially an agrarian game, designed to give everyone a go. What is rather good about cricket is that it requires the minimum of effort over the maximum amount of time.

Not that much different from working for the Public Service, really. The game doesn't start till about ten, there's a lot of standing around, a fair amount of gossip and rivalry, people break for lunch and tea, and as soon as conditions aren't just ideal, everyone stops.

A friend, new to Australia, after hearing a great deal about the game but never having seen it played, insisted that friends take him along to a match. Once installed in his seat, he ate and drank with his friends, oblivious of the passage of time. Towards late afternoon, however, when the food and beer were beginning to run out, he turned to his friends and said with polite but casual curiosity:

"So tell me, when is this game going to start?"

Fortunately most of the boredom of cricket, for the players at least, has been removed nowadays by widening the game to include the drinking of beer and heavy intoxicating liquor on Australian television commercials.

So as long as you are reasonably intact, without visible

A Public Service sort of a game

signs of cerebral palsy, and can stand up for seven or eight hours without falling asleep (a ball will fly past you every now and then), your chances of making it through the game are fairly good.

If you also happen to be fairly dull, well-behaved, and have the stomach to drink with the more influential cricket team selectors, your chances of becoming captain of the side are even better.

Should you be willing to forget the inconveniences of travel, or those of standing in a field somewhere in England, the Caribbean or Asia — hoping that whatever flies towards you is a ball and not a bomb — you might in fact become a cricket great, adored by hundreds of thousands of screaming fans.

Patience, after all, makes many things possible. Even becoming a great Australian.